STEM
Waterworks

How Do RESERVOIRS Work?

Therese Shea

PowerKiDS
press.

New York

Published in 2017 by The Rosen Publishing Group, Inc.
29 East 21st Street, New York, NY 10010

First Edition

Editor: Greg Roza
Book Design: Mickey Harmon

Photo Credits: Cover, pp. 1–32 (water) elic/Shutterstock.com; cover, pp. 1–32 (pipes) Kovalenko Alexander/Shutterstock.com; cover (image) Pete Mcbride/National Geographic Magazines/Getty Images; p. 5 Det-anan/Shutterstock.com; p. 7 (inset) Ms Deborah Waters/Shutterstock.com; p. 7 (inset) kao/ Shutterstock.com; p. 7 Jason Edwards/National Geographic Magazines/Getty Images; p. 9 Steven Hockney/Shutterstock.com; p. 11 pau2000/Shutterstock.com; p. 13 Bildagentur Zoonar GmbH/Shutterstock.com; p. 15 Robert Hoetink/Shutterstock.com; p. 17 Planet Observer/Universal Images Group/Getty Images; p. 19 Goodluz/Shutterstock.com; p. 21 Richard Thornton/Shutterstock.com; p. 23 Budmir Jevtic/Shutterstock.com; p. 25 Irfan Khan/Contributor/Getty Images; p. 27 Disability Images/Getty Images; p. 29 Jerry Horbert/Shutterstock.com.

Library of Congress Cataloging-in-Publication Data

Names: Shea, Therese, author.
Title: How do reservoirs work? / Therese Shea.
Description: New York : PowerKids Press, [2017] | Series: STEM waterworks |
   Includes index.
Identifiers: LCCN 2015047768 | ISBN 9781499420111 (pbk.) | ISBN 9781499420135 (library bound) | ISBN 9781499420128 (6 pack)
Subjects: LCSH: Reservoirs–Juvenile literature. | Water-supply–Juvenile
   literature.
Classification: LCC TC530 .S54 2017 | DDC 627.86–dc23
LC record available at http://lccn.loc.gov/2015047768

Manufactured in the United States of America

CPSIA Compliance Information: Batch #BS16PK: For Further Information contact Rosen Publishing, New York, New York at 1-800-237-9932

Contents

Wanted: Water

Imagine you live far from water, in an area where it hardly ever rains. How would you get the water you need to drink, bathe, or even put out a fire?

People have long adapted their **environment** to their way of life. They build houses that keep them warm in winter and cool in summer. They construct bridges that cross canyons. They remove forests to erect cities and dig tunnels through mountains! So, what do they do about a lack of water?

This is the kind of problem that scientists and engineers love to tackle. Building a reservoir—a man-made lake—isn't easy. It takes STEM skills. "STEM" stands for "science, technology, engineering, and math." Constructing a reservoir that meets the needs of a community requires knowledge of each of these subjects.

In the Pipe

Different kinds of engineers plan, construct, and maintain reservoirs. Civil engineers build structures such as bridges and dams. Water engineers are civil engineers who focus on structures that deal with water.

A reservoir and a lake can look much alike. Some reservoirs are even called lakes. So, what's the difference? A reservoir is man-made. This photo shows the reservoir called Lake Powell on the Colorado River.

Many people around the world rely on a supply of freshwater year round. Others need a dependable supply at certain times of the year, such as during a dry summer, but have too much water at other periods, such as during a rainy spring.

Many reservoirs built today serve more than one purpose. Reservoirs provide a dependable water source for many needs and wants, including drinking, washing, irrigating crops, firefighting, and swimming. Some reservoirs are created for the simple purpose of recreation. They're places for people to boat, fish, and swim. Reservoirs can also make sure floodwaters are contained or redirected, so they're less likely to harm property and threaten lives.

In the Pipe

Water naturally flows downhill because of gravity, which helps water systems function. Some reservoirs are built in low places so water can flow into them. When people need to move water uphill, they use pumps.

Overflowing floodwaters can escape from a reservoir in several ways. Here are three designs, called spillways, that deal with overflow in reservoirs.

Service Reservoirs

Service reservoirs are closed containers of steel or concrete. They're designed to hold water that's been cleaned and prepared for people's use. Service reservoirs can be found underground or partially underground in higher areas. Some service reservoirs are in water towers. An elevated location is important. The force of gravity is needed to create enough pressure to push the water down through pipes to its destination. Sometimes pumps are needed to provide extra force.

Service reservoirs have several functions, including acting as a source of water for emergencies and keeping the water supply of a community steady during periods of high demand. When a community's usual water **distribution** system isn't enough, water flows out of the service reservoir. It's later replaced and maintained until it's needed again.

Service reservoirs are also called cisterns. Each may hold about a day's worth of water for a community.

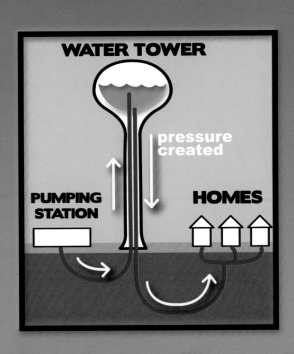

WATER TOWER

pressure created

PUMPING STATION

HOMES

In the Pipe

If a service reservoir holds extra water, where does a community normally get its water? Groundwater, lakes, rivers, and large reservoirs are the sources for most communities. About 98 percent of Earth's liquid freshwater exists as groundwater!

Embankment Reservoirs

The path of a stream or river can be diverted, or changed, to place water into a **depression**, which may be natural or man-made. This process forms an embankment reservoir, which is sometimes called a bankside or bounded reservoir.

For man-made embankment reservoirs, an area of land is hollowed out. Then, an embankment, or ridge, of earth or stone is built around the depression to help contain the water. Smaller reservoirs may be lined with a material, sometimes clay, that keeps water from seeping into the ground. Finally, water is diverted into the reservoir through pipes or canals using gravity or pumps. The amount of water in embankment reservoirs can be changed by allowing more water from the sources to flow into the reservoir or by allowing water to flow out of the reservoir.

Over a period of time, natural processes clean water in an open reservoir like this embankment reservoir. However, if it's intended for drinking, the water will be treated before it reaches people's homes.

Valley-Dammed Reservoirs

In some locations, nature provides the embankment for a reservoir. A valley-dammed reservoir (or valley reservoir) is the result when a dam is built across a river flowing though a narrow valley. The water that would normally flow downstream backs up, creating a lake contained by the dam and the sides of the valley. Should the reservoir become too full, water may be released through pipes, canals, or spillways. The amount of water released into the valley below can be controlled.

Some dams are constructed with a hydroelectric power plant to produce electricity. This kind of power plant uses the force of the water passing through the dam to turn the blades of **turbines**. The moving blades provide the mechanical energy **generators** need to produce electricity.

In the Pipe

Before a dam can be built across a river, the river must be diverted away from the construction site, often through tunnels. After construction is complete, the tunnels are removed, and the water fills up the reservoir.

Valley-dammed reservoirs are the largest reservoirs. Engineers use the natural landscape of the area as walls for the reservoir.

Ancient Engineering

People have been making reservoirs for thousands of years. The oldest surviving dam in the world—constructed of rock and earth—was built around 3000 BC! Located in the Black Desert of modern-day Jordan, the Jawa Dam's reservoir stored water from a stream that was used to irrigate nearby farmland.

In 2010, archaeologists found the remains of two reservoirs in ancient Maya ruins in a Mexican rain forest. They discovered one of the man-made lake beds had been lined with pieces of **ceramic** to prevent water from seeping into the ground. These pools, called *aguadas*, are probably about 1,500 years old and are as large as eight Olympic-size swimming pools. The Maya experienced a dry season of about three months each year, so a reserve of water was important.

Reservoirs are particularly necessary in regions that don't receive a lot of rainfall each year. This ancient reservoir was part of a larger system in the Khirbat Qumran region of Israel.

Reservoirs Today

Modern engineers have constructed some truly incredible reservoirs. Lake Volta in Ghana, Africa—formed from the damming of the Volta River—is the largest reservoir in the world by surface area. It covers about 3,280 square miles (8,495 sq km).

The largest reservoir by volume is Lake Kariba, which lies between the African countries of Zambia and Zimbabwe. This body was formed by damming the Zambezi River. Its volume is 44 cubic miles (183 cu km), or over 48 trillion gallons (182 trillion L).

In the Pipe

In the late 1800s, the largest U.S. reservoir, Lake Conemaugh, was located in Pennsylvania. When its dam collapsed in 1889, 3.6 billion gallons (13.6 billion L) of water swept away the town of Johnstown, Pennsylvania, killing 2,209 people.

Lake Volta is visible from space. This reservoir is larger than the state of Delaware!

In the United States, the Hoover Dam was built across the Colorado River at the border of Arizona and Nevada to create Lake Mead—the largest reservoir in the nation. The reservoir and the dam's hydroelectric power plant provide a water supply, flood control, irrigation, and electricity.

Reservoirs from Start to Finish

The massive dimensions of some reservoirs—and disasters like the one that occurred at Johnstown—demand that such bodies of water be carefully planned. Engineers, scientists, and other workers consider many issues before building begins. These workers frequently use science, technology, engineering, and math.

For example, the plant and animal life of the proposed site must be studied closely. Environmental planners try to determine the positive and negative effects on local species. The reservoir's water source is examined for **sediment** and pollution. Systems may be put in place to make it safe for human use.

Scientists must also consider how weather and climate will affect the reservoir. They must figure out ways to keep the water level steady no matter how much (or how little) **precipitation** the area receives.

Scientists may use special atoms, called isotope tracers, to study the movement of water in a reservoir or through a dam.

Before building a reservoir, engineers use math to calculate how much water is needed. They consider how the water will be used by the community.

For example, a reservoir may be built to store water for fighting fires. It's estimated that firefighters may need about 500 gallons (1,892 L) per minute over two hours to put out a fire in a community of single-family houses. This requires a reservoir holding about 60,000 gallons (227,124 L). But in an area with many businesses, 4,000 gallons (15,141 L) per minute over four hours may be needed to fight fires. A reservoir of 960,000 gallons (3.6 million L) of water is suggested.

If the reservoir is used for more than one purpose, such as for irrigation and firefighting, the volume of water needed for each purpose is added together.

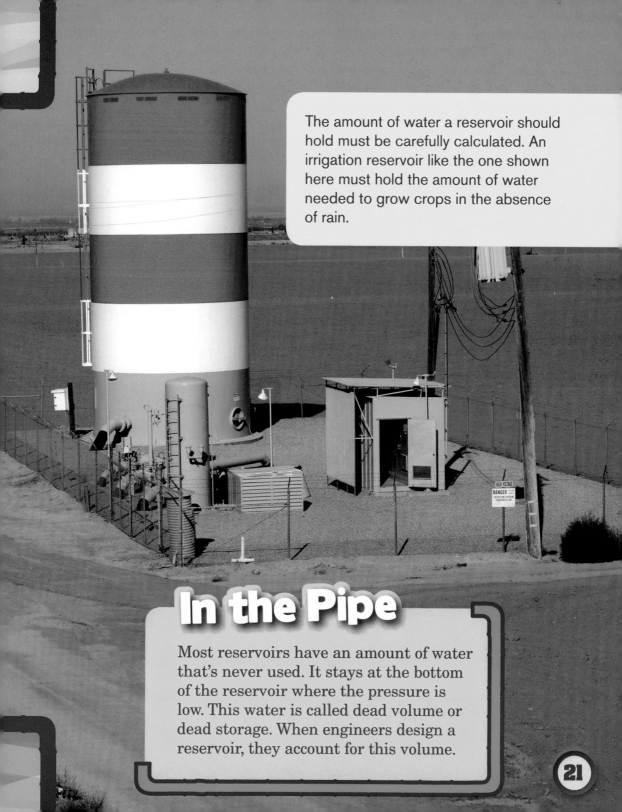

The amount of water a reservoir should hold must be carefully calculated. An irrigation reservoir like the one shown here must hold the amount of water needed to grow crops in the absence of rain.

In the Pipe

Most reservoirs have an amount of water that's never used. It stays at the bottom of the reservoir where the pressure is low. This water is called dead volume or dead storage. When engineers design a reservoir, they account for this volume.

Engineers use multiple kinds of technology in the construction of reservoirs. Machines such as excavators are used to dig out and scrape the land for valley-dammed and embankment reservoirs. Engineers test linings and use the best ones to prevent percolation into rocks and soil in smaller reservoirs. Service reservoirs used to store drinking water are lined with materials such as rubber and plastic to prevent **contamination**.

Engineers may place pumps in areas where force is needed to continue the flow of the water to a location. They use pipes, tunnels, or canals in places where water needs to travel to and from the reservoir. Computers help monitor water levels after construction. And—in the case of dams with attached power plants—turbines, generators, and other technology are used to produce, store, and transport electrical power.

Smaller reservoirs are lined to prevent percolation, or the process of water passing into the ground below. It's too expensive to line large reservoirs, however, so a certain amount of water is lost each year through percolation.

Evaporation Setbacks and Solutions

Even a well-constructed and maintained reservoir experiences changing water levels. Rain and melting snow can add great volume to a body of water. Besides percolation, a major cause of water loss is evaporation. In some deserts, a reservoir may lose up to 5 feet (1.5 m) of water or more a year. Little precipitation can be expected to take its place.

Engineers and scientists are always looking for ways to make better reservoirs. In Saudi Arabia, builders covered a reservoir with mats made of leaves, which greatly slowed the rate of evaporation.

In Los Angeles, California, three reservoirs were covered with millions of plastic balls, called "shade balls," in 2015. It's thought the shade balls could prevent the reservoirs from losing 300 million gallons (1.1 billion L) of water to evaporation annually.

The shade balls in the Los Angeles reservoirs also shield the water from dust and wildlife. They disrupt the formation of bromate, which is a toxic substance that can develop after adding **chlorine** to water in an effort to make the water suitable for drinking.

Settling Sediment

River water flowing into a reservoir carries sediment. The tiny bits of sand, rock, and dirt settle in the reservoir and build up over time. This takes up space and cuts down on the amount of water the reservoir can hold. Sediment can also harm hydroelectric power equipment and reduce the amount of electricity produced.

Though sediment can be removed from reservoirs, it's a costly process. Some dams are constructed with gates that can be opened to release some sediment.

Many dams have been built without a plan for removing sediment. Instead, the reservoirs were planned with some sediment buildup expected. However, even the largest reservoirs may only be useful for about 100 years because of sediment.

In the Pipe

Farming and building contribute to sediment buildup in reservoirs because they loosen the top layer of soil. Planting forests is one way to cut down on sediment buildup. Trees and other plants keep soil in place.

precipitation

evaporation

reservoir

dam

sediment

Engineers may use boats with **sonar** and **lidar** to investigate sediment buildup in reservoirs. This water engineer uses a special scope to observe the sediment floating in the water.

Environmental Impact

The environmental impact of a large reservoir is substantial. It displaces plants and animals. It attracts people who want to live or build businesses nearby, which further disrupts the natural environment. Further, the building of dams and reservoirs can upset the migration routes of fish and change the temperature, depth, currents, and oxygen levels of the rivers.

It's the law in many countries that the proposed site for a reservoir must be studied carefully with the environmental consequences in mind. If the effects will be too harmful for the area, the reservoir may never be built. However, the needs of a community are sometimes considered more important than the needs of the environment. Providing water for a community often disrupts the environment around it.

An engineer takes photos of a swamp located near a reservoir to monitor the reservoir's effects on the wetland.

In the Pipe

Another problem with some reservoirs is the formation of algae blooms. These growths can make river water poisonous for fish and people. Dams along the Klamath River in California caused algae blooms that resulted in the death of many fish and water too dangerous for people to swim in.

Yet another danger attributed to reservoirs may be surprising to you. Some scientists believe they can trigger earthquakes! The tremendous water pressure created by large reservoirs may force water into small cracks in the ground and cause the plates on which Earth's surface rests to slip, resulting in an earthquake.

Reservoirs have allowed people to live in places where they otherwise couldn't survive. However, the many negative effects on the surrounding environment can't be ignored. In the future, scientists and engineers will focus on less harmful ways of supplying water to people. They'll recycle and reuse wastewater to fulfill irrigation and fire protection needs. They'll likely build more underground reservoirs to avoid evaporation, pollution, and displacing plants and animals. Can you think of more ways to engineer a better reservoir?

Glossary

ceramic: An object made of clay that is then heated to a very high temperature so that it hardens.

chlorine: A chemical element sometimes used to disinfect and deodorize.

contamination: The process of making something dangerous, dirty, or impure by adding something harmful to it.

depression: An area that dips lower than the surface surrounding it, forming a "bowl" where water can gather.

distribution: Having to do with the way something is shared or spread out.

environment: The natural world in which a plant or animal lives.

generator: A machine that uses movement to produce electricity.

lidar: A device that releases pulses of laser light to detect an object's location, movement, and speed.

precipitation: Water that falls to the ground as hail, mist, rain, sleet, or snow.

sediment: Matter such as rocks, sand, and stones that is moved and deposited by water, wind, or glaciers.

sonar: A device that uses echoes to locate objects.

turbine: An engine with blades that are caused to spin by the movement of water, steam, or air.

Index

Websites

Due to the changing nature of Internet links, PowerKids Press has developed an online list of websites related to the subject of this book. This site is updated regularly. Please use this link to access the list: www.powerkidslinks.com/sww/res